NEW ZEAI

THE NORTH IS

Photography by Mike Clare
Text by John Dunmore

TIMES EDITIONS

Contents

Maui's Fish

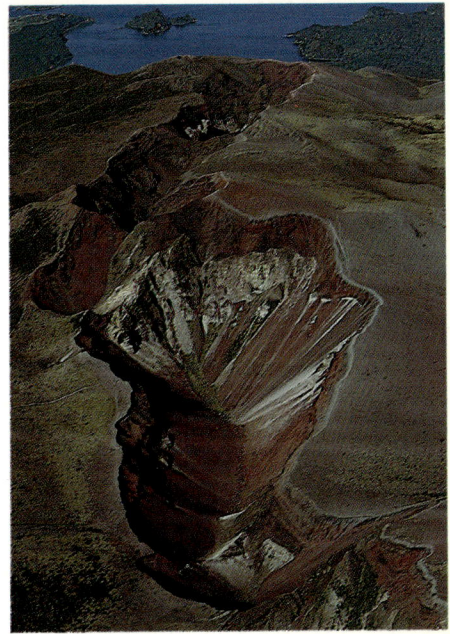

Many are the tales they tell of Maui, the son of the goddess Matanga, but none is better known than the story of his fishing up the North Island.

The Maoris called him Maui-the-wise, but other Polynesians knew him as Maui-of-a-thousand-tricks. He was an impish, gifted god. There are stories of how he snared the sun, controlled the winds, re-arranged the stars, turned his brother-in-law into a dog, and stole his grandmother's jawbone.

When his brothers went out on a fishing expedition, Maui decided to go along with them to see what other wonders he might perform.

His brothers, jealous of his magical powers, had not wanted him to go on this fishing expedition, so he hid in their canoe until they were far out at sea and no longer in sight of land. Even then, they would not allow him to use his line with the magic hook, claiming they had gone quite far enough and that their catch was entirely sufficient for their needs.

Maui urged them to sail further and yet further into unknown waters and then he insisted on being allowed to fish. They refused him a share of their bait, so he struck himself violently on the nose and baited his hook with his own blood.

His line went over the side of the canoe and down into the kingdom of Tangaroa, the sea god, where it caught a great fish which came up to the surface, threshing and struggling. Maui warned his brothers not to touch it until he had made the appropriate prayers and offering to the gods, but again they refused to listen to him and set upon it.

And to this day the land bears the scars and the jagged marks of their impiety: the bites into the coastline, the deep furrows of the valleys along the spine of the mountain ranges.

For this is the North Island, *Te Ika na Maui*, the Fish of Maui. And indeed the island looks like a mighty fish, a giant manta ray with its mouth at Wellington harbour, its long tail stretching north and the wide gash of Hawke Bay where Maui's hook caught it.

Preceding pages: The North Island's highest mountain and still an active volcano, Mt Ruapehu stretches its arms protectively over the resting sheep.

Left: Like silver water, Lake Waikaremoana glistens in the Urewera Ranges. Above: Viewed from the air the mountain looks as though it had been split asunder by the mighty hands of an angry giant.

7

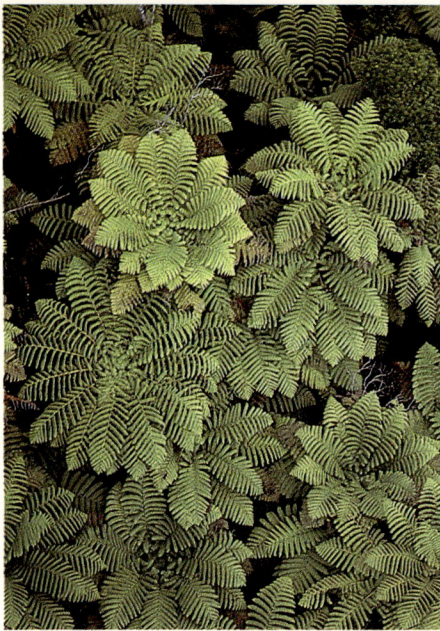

The island certainly rose from the sea millions of years ago in a long series of great volcanic struggles which are not over yet, for the volcanoes still fume and the earth still shakes like a great slumbering beast.

It stretches in a curve almost a thousand kilometres long from Cape Reinga in the north to Cape Palliser in the south and consequently encompasses a wide variety of climates and flora.

The north is semi-tropical, with citrus fruit and mangrove swamps, the centre lush, rich pastures, the home of dairy herds and world-famous horseracing studs, the south is temperate and bracing but often lashed by wild southerly storms that sometimes roar through Cook Strait.

Although it was a late starter — in the nineteenth century, the South Island seemed the more promising of the two — the North Island has more people, well over 70 percent of the population, living there and nearly 40 percent of all New Zealanders have their home in the two largest cities, Auckland and Wellington. Yet it is much the smaller of the two islands, being only 114,450 sq.km as compared with the 150,700 sq.km of the South Island.

The North Island not only has the capital, Wellington, and populous Auckland, but also most of the head offices of the country's major businesses.

Its products reflect the wide range of an economy still mainly based on agriculture — there are dairy and sheep farms, vineyards, orchards containing acres of the wonder kiwifruit — but now increasingly developing an industrial base, for each of the main towns is ringed with new factories and few are the small centres which do not boast at least a factory or two.

It has snow-capped volcanoes, some still smoking, others now silent. It boasts the longest river, the Waikato, the largest lake, Taupo, the hottest island, White Island where rocks glow dull red and cracks in the soil attain a temperature of 850 to 900 degrees Celsius, and an entire wonderland of boiling mud pools and geysers where steam from the earth heats houses and provides electric power.

Maui's fish is no dead world. It breathes and moves, but contentedly, protective towards those who have made their home on its scarred but still magical back.

Discoverers — Old and New

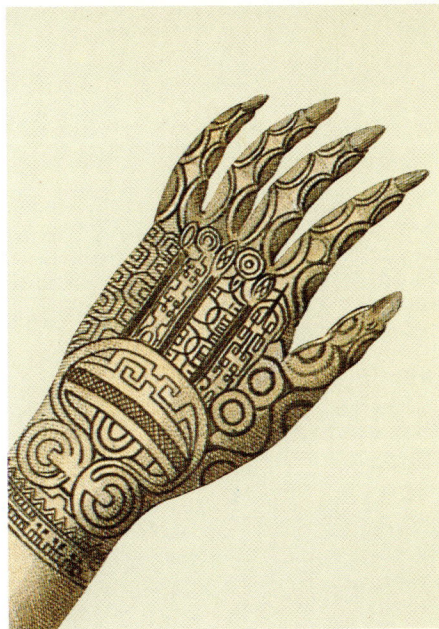

"Vikings of the Sunrise", one of their own people, the great anthropologist Te Rangi Hiroa, once called them.

During Europe's Dark Ages when men feared to travel beyond their village or sail out of sight of a familiar coast, the Polynesians went from island to island in their double canoes, as far as Hawaii in the north, Easter Island in the east, and at last to New Zealand in the south-west.

It was Kupe, the legend tells us, fleeing from the angry family of a man with whose wife he had run away, who discovered New Zealand, circumnavigated the islands and returned home with news of his great discovery. No other Polynesian hero is recorded in the ancient tales as having made the journey back to his distant and legendary homeland, Hawaiki, from the place they called Aotearoa — the Land of the Long White Cloud — for thus it had appeared, spread along the far southern horizon.

The great land was uninhabited, covered in dense forests broken here and there by wide expanses of plains where strange flightless birds roamed; the *moa*, as tall as a man, some taller. The rivers and the seas teemed with fish. The soil was rich. The climate was mild. It was indeed a paradise on earth.

A great fleet of canoes set out for the new land. Canoes lashed together and decked over, with great plaited sails, handled with great dexterity by the master navigators of the Pacific who could read the stars as easily as a mariner could read a chart.

Whole families came, with their utensils, fishing hooks, crops, their dogs even and, unwelcome hidden guests, the rats. They settled on the island, each great canoe with its historic landfall to serve as a reminder of their origins and to be the focus of their tribal pride. Unlike Kupe, they did not return. One did not visit relatives one had farewelled before the great departure, and if others were to follow they could do so by following directions Kupe had laid down.

The Great Migration has been discounted by those who came much later, with their carbon-dating and their scientific methods, proving that New Zealand had

Preceding pages: A Maori canoe race in Auckland, nineteenth century steel engraving (Courtesy Antiques of the Orient, Singapore). Left: Early European impressions of Maori tattoos. Handtinted steel engraving (Courtesy Antiques of the Orient, Singapore). Once they learnt that Maori chiefs were elaborately tattooed, European artists let their imagination run free, as they frequently did when interpreting landscapes and scenes of the Pacific. But tattooing was a slow and painful process and it would technically have been impossible to produce such designs as appear on the hand (above).

been settled much earlier than the year 1350 which early scholars, piecing together Maori history out of legends and old family traditions, had laid down as the date when the Great Fleet arrived.

But if there had been no Great Fleet, no organised migration, the result was much the same. The Maoris settled, multiplied, prospered, evolved a complex culture, adapting their ancient Polynesian traditions to the new environment.

They built fortified villages on cliffs and hills, *pas* defended by complex lines of palisades — for tribes and sub-tribes were often at war. Family links were close, imposing duties and responsibilities on everyone, binding them in an intricate network of protective and supportive customs.

The *tapu* (taboo) could protect a crop or control an unruly warrior. The chief had the power but he was only the trustee of the tribe. He did not own land nor fishing grounds and although he could allow others to have access to them, he could not sell them. It was something the European, when he arrived with his long tradition of private ownership, of buying and selling, took many years to understand.

With colonisation, the people of the land, the *tangata whenua*, gradually lost their sense of belonging; their numbers fell until, by the end of the century, writers spoke of a doomed race. But resilience and adaptability saved them. The people of the land survived.

Their numbers grew again. Today although nearly all have also a European ancestry and mixed marriages are still frequent, they represent over 9 percent of New Zealand's population.

The first of the non-Polynesian explorers was a Dutchman called Abel Tasman, in 1642. Attacked by a war party of Maoris in canoes, Tasman did not stay, and all was quiet for more than a century, until James Cook's arrival off the east coast in 1769.

Cook was to circumnavigate and chart New Zealand, coming back on several occasions, and to make the country and its people known to Europe. The French came too, Surville anchored in Doubtless Bay in the far north in 1769 and Marion du Fresne put in at the Bay of Islands three years later.

It was the beginning of an irreversible transforma-

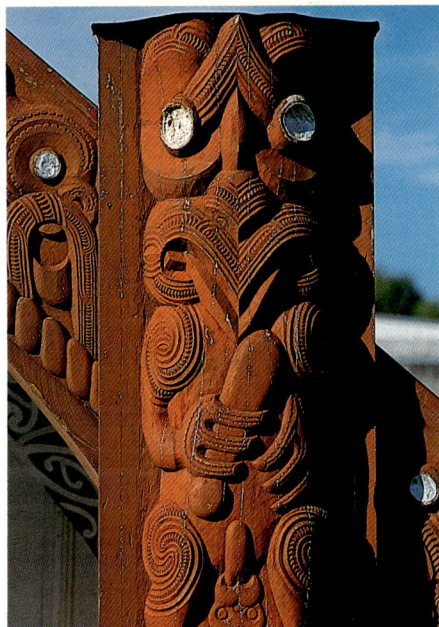

Left and above: *Carvings from the Putiki marae, Wanganui River. Maori carvings are filled with symbolic meaning and many of them recall tribal history or famous ancestors.*

17

Right: The signing of the Treaty of Waitangi, 1840. This reconstruction of the scene by Leonard C. Mitchell is the most accurate impression yet painted, although some artistic licence has crept in. (Cover from the N.Z. Journal of Agriculture, January 1949, reproduced by courtesy of the Alexander Turnbull Library, Wellington). Above: Signatures of chiefs not present at the official signing of the treaty were collected in May 1840 by missionaries Henry Williams and Octavius Hadfield. Most chiefs signed by reproducing their "moko" or personal tattoo.

tion. The Bay of Islands became a regular port of call for whalers, sealers and traders. Sheltered, warm, with charming inlets and beaches, the Bay welcomed the first permanent white settlers — missionaries, merchants, tavern keepers, farmers. In time, Britain sent a Resident, James Busby, and in 1840 came Captain William Hobson to raise the British flag and found the new colony.

It was in the Bay of Islands that the Treaty of Waitangi was signed. Difficult though it was to translate into Maori such term as 'sovereignty' and 'governor', it gave the various tribes protection from unscrupulous exploiters and kept away other European powers with designs on the country.

Colonists were sent out by the New Zealand Company, a private semi-commercial organisation promoted by Edward Gibbon Wakefield who had earlier been imprisoned for eloping with a young heiress — one is reminded of Kupe's flight to New Zealand after a comparable marital entanglement.

The colonists settled mostly along the coasts of Wellington, New Plymouth, Auckland, Wanganui. But as communications improved, they moved further inland, buying land through the government, felling the bush, establishing farms and townships and gradually creating organised communities.

Inevitably, there were serious clashes with the Maoris whose concept of land ownership was quite different and who had insufficient time to adapt to new farming methods. There were many incidents between the old residents and the new, neither of whom understood the other's way of life.

Roads and bridges helped to open up the land right to the foothills of the great ranges. Then railway lines snaked across the plains and the river flats, spanning the ravines and the gorges with viaducts that are even now wonders of engineering skill.

The ports were deepened and widened. Sail had soon given way to steam, while refrigerated cargo ships capable of taking frozen lamb and dairy products across the world further transformed the economy and with it the country and its pioneering way of life.

The population reached one million after 70 years; two million 45 years after that; but it took a mere 20 years more to reach the third million.

Above: *The valuable feather cloak or "kaitaka".*
Right: *Traditional wood carving is a skill passed on from one generation to the next and surrounded by deep mystical significance.*

The Big Smoke

The Largest Polynesian City in the World

When the French explorer Dumont d'Urville first sailed into the waters of the Waitemata in February 1827 he was struck by its potential as a harbour. Deep water everywhere, sheltered coves, green forested hills. Maori canoes paddled around him, but the place looked almost deserted. Inland, however, on hilltops and headlands, there was a large Maori population, possibly up to 20,000.

After the 1840 colonisation, its excellence as a harbour was soon recognised. The new Lieutenant-Governor, William Hobson, realising that the Bay of Islands was more picturesque than useful as an administrative centre, established his capital there and named the fledgling settlement Auckland after his superior, the Earl of Auckland, First Lord of the Admiralty. It showed courage as well as foresight, for at the time the total European population numbered two.

Auckland subsequently lost its status as a capital, but it remains the largest city, the most cosmopolitan, the most lively. Its semi-tropical climate makes it an outdoor city, exemplified by its sports grounds, its golf courses, its yacht marinas, the architecture of its houses open to the sun or set in the bush, but perhaps most dramatically by the famous annual Round-the-Bays Run when some 80,000 Aucklanders take to the roads in one great fun-filled marathon.

The love of the open air has led to Auckland extending ever further as her people go out in search of a piece of land that can provide a garden, with space for a tennis court or easy access to a bay, which means it now stretches for more than 30 kilometres from north to south, its homes spreading along the curve of the bay and over the hills — which in fact are extinct volcanoes — all 63 of them.

The country's largest seaport and the largest industrial centre, Auckland has also the busiest international airport. It is the gateway to Asia, to America and to the islands of the Pacific. Entry point therefore for immigrants from the islands, it offers a climate that appeals to

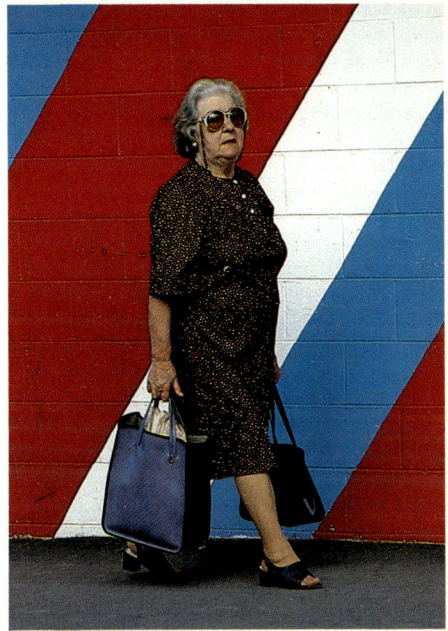

Preceding pages: Waitangi Festival, Waitangi. The women in (modern) traditional costume, are displaying their skill in a "poi" dance, the poi being a ball of some light material tied with flax.

Left: *A mixture of old and new marks this view of the Auckland waterfront. Although the bridge now spans the harbour, ferries still ply to some parts of the north shore, bringing commuters into the city in a matter of minutes.* **Above:** *Modern art may brighten the scene, but it does not necessarily lighten shopping bags.*

Polynesians, with good opportunities for employment. Over the years, Cook Islanders, Tokelau Islanders, Samoans, Tongans have made Auckland their home and given the city streets their distinctive flavour.

The process is still going on, but Auckland has already earned the title of the largest Polynesian city in the world. The statistics are impressive: although Auckland City itself, the area controlled by the Auckland City Council, has only 150,000 inhabitants, the Auckland urban district is rapidly approaching the 900,000 mark, and the ethnic composition is: European 81 percent, New Zealand Maoris 6 percent, Pacific Islanders 9 percent, others 4 percent.

Fate has made Auckland cosmopolitan, since it is open to both the Tasman Sea and the Pacific Ocean, which are separated only by a narrow isthmus — so narrow in fact, that one hapless nineteenth-century merchant captain sailed into the shallows of the western Manukau Harbour expecting to pass through into

Preceding pages: The tremendous growth and development of Auckland is visible in this view of the downtown area. **Below and right:** *The old and the new. The Auckland skyline displays its modern buildings and the cranes ceaselessly at work on new tower blocks, but a closer look* (**above right**) *shows how the leisurely traditions of the city and the loved old buildings have survived in the modern age.*

Auckland Harbour. The isthmus area is called *Tamaki-makau-rau*, "the spouse fought over by a hundred lovers". It reflects the early history and endless struggles that went on for control of this strategic region.

The battles have long since come to an end, but Tamaki is still besieged by her hundred lovers, who have come from all parts of the Pacific, from distant Europe, from India and China, to enjoy the beauty of her bays and beaches and to lay siege to her heart.

Skyscrapers on the Beach

When Whatonga was competing in the great canoe races at Pikopikoiwhiti, in faraway Hawaiki, a sudden storm blew up and scattered the contestants. His heart-broken grandfather, Toi, set out in search of him.

This, they say, happened in the twelfth century. Toi searched the furthest seas and came to New Zealand where he sailed into a vast landlocked harbour which

Auckland street scenes. The largest city, prosperous but never straitlaced, Auckland displays its **joie de vivre** *and its eminently practical style of dress.*

he called *Whanganui a Tara* — the Great Harbour of Tara — after his eldest son.

In time the white man discovered it, not easily because its entrance is relatively narrow, and named it Port Nicholson, after the harbourmaster of Sydney, New South Wales. Officially, it still retains that name, but it is known today as Wellington Harbour.

The first settlers came in 1840 and were attracted by the beach at Petone and the low lands by the Hutt river, but the river was given to unpredictable floodings and the settlers moved across the bay to the beach and rising hills of Wellington. A bank had already opened a branch at Petone and it was also forced to relocate. John Smith, the manager, was rowed across on a raft, sitting on top of his safe and was thereafter known as "Jackie Box Smith".

There was little flat land for homes or warehouses. An enterprising businessman ran the wrecked hull of a ship onto the beach and used it as a wharf, a warehouse and an office; but one would look in vain today for this famous "Plimmer's Ark" among the tower blocks.

Few of the many thousands who throng the shopping and financial centre of Wellington today spare even a fleeting thought for the fact that beneath their feet was once a pebbled beach or indeed that above them was once the high water mark. Cellars used to flood in old Wellington when the tide was particularly high. But those days are now forgotten for the city lies close to a major faultline, and new building regulations have led to the rebuilding of most of the downtown area.

Wellington became the capital in 1865, much to Auckland's dismay. It was agreed that a more central location was needed, but to avoid an open breach between the two cities, a commission of Australians was invited to select a site for New Zealand's capital. Their terms of reference limited their choice to the Cook Strait area, so with due solemnity they nominated Wellington as the capital city.

Parliamentary Buildings in neo-Gothic style were built but never completed. Lack of space forced a decision in the 1960s and the English architect Sir Basil Spence recommended a total departure from the traditional style. The Beehive is now a distinctive feature of the Wellington skyline.

Preceding pages: *Auckland's Anniversary Regatta Day brings out a host of small craft on Waitemata Harbour, but they are dwarfed by the size of the harbour and the great Harbour Bridge.*
Left: *Between St Gerard's Monastery and Wellington's financial centre — some might say between God and Mammon — an inter-island ferry pauses at the Overseas Terminal.* Above: *The "Beehive", which houses ministerial offices. Built after a suggested design by the British architect Sir Basil Spence, it was completed in 1980.*

Preceding pages: *Young fishermen near Oriental Bay, Wellington.* **Right:** *The eye of the expert. After decades of traditional Anglo-Saxon recipes, New Zealanders have enthusiastically taken to all kinds of European and American foods.*

Right: *The largest wooden building in the southern hemisphere, Government Buildings, Wellington, built in 1876 and now lovingly restored down to its smallest details* (**above left**). *The building has been designed to give the impression of stonework so that it can be called a masterpiece of architectural* **trompe-l'oeil.**

The Far North

Hine-te-Aparangi, the wife of Kupe the navigator, had wearied of the long days at sea, when she sighted a white cloud lying over the horizon. "He ao", she called out, "a cloud". "Ao-tea-roa", others then shouted, "a long white cloud".

They had sighted the edge of the North Island, which became known as the Land of the Long White Cloud, a name which in time was applied to New Zealand.

The Far North is filled with legends and traditions. It is from the very tip of the northern peninsula, Cape Reinga, that the spirits of the dead leap into the sea to begin their journey to their magic homeland, Hawaiki. Tourists come now in busloads to view it and the great *Pohutukawa* tree, imbued with sacred myths, that clings to the cliff edge.

They travel mostly along the vast stretch of beach on the western shore, Ninety Mile Beach (it is nearer 60 miles, but who is counting?) because this is — or was until recently — the Roadless North, a quiet, warm, hospitable land, isolated from the turmoil and business of Auckland, 250 km to the south.

You may pass by Hokianga, a peaceful waterway, and see the statue of the boy and the dolphin at Opononi beach: you are too late to see Opo himself, a well-loved dolphin who made the Hokianga his home back in the 1950s and who was protected by a special Order-in-Council.

Travelling south from the Hokianga one reaches the Waipoua kauri forest, where the mighty *Agathis australis* still grows, including Tane Mahuta, with a girth of 17.3 metres, reputed to be more than 2,000 years old. Looking up at it in this great tree, awesome in the virgin bush, one realises why the ancient Maori honoured Tane, the god of the forests, the primeval force in the mystery of creation.

On the east coast one cannot miss the Bay of Islands, so named by James Cook in 1769 from the number of bush-clad islands that fill it, peaceful havens for myriads of birds and the occasional Maori settlement.

It is replete with history. Here the first missionaries landed; here Captain Hobson read his proclamation,

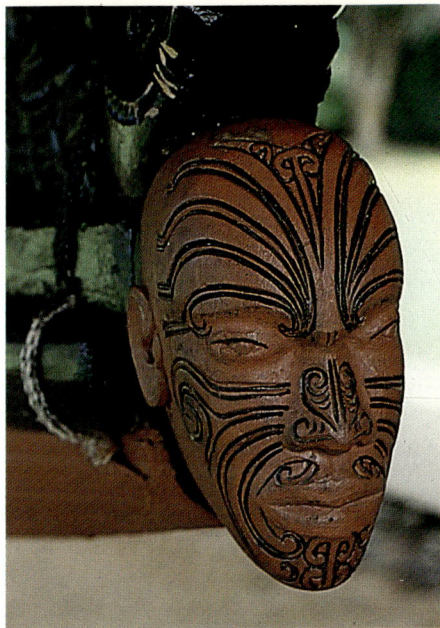

Preceding pages: A quiet haven near the centre of Wellington, dominated by St Gerard's Monastery and homes crowding together for a glimpse of the large and beautiful harbour beyond.

Left: A flotilla of yachts slumbers in a quiet cove, Bay of Islands. Above: Detail of a war canoe, Waitangi, showing the facial tattoo or "moko".

and here, near the quiet little town of Russell, Hone Heke the Maori Chief, repeatedly cut down the flagstaff with its Union Jack, the symbol of British power. Governor Fitzroy offered a reward of £100 for the capture of the troublesome chief, and the next day Heke offered £100 for the capture of the governor.

Today tourists pour in to tour the bay in launches, for a leisurely and inexpensive lunch of champagne and chicken in the shelter of a quiet bay, or for the more extensive "cream run" past isolated farms on lonely headlands. Others venture further out in search of the deep sea marlin and the mako shark. Some make for the hills or the virgin bush; others retrace history in old churches, at the Treaty House or in the Old Stone Store at Kerikeri. Many step aboard the *Tui*, to visit the Museum of Shipwrecks, where the decks heave and the endless sound of the sea is recreated in eerie darkness.

Once a roadless and sleepy place, the Far North has now leapt into the twentieth century: the thriving port

The challenge of the future, the wisdom of the past.
Below: *Darryl and Taumatariki, at Mokau, Bay of Islands.* **Right:** *Stan Booth examines one of the juicy oranges for which his home town of Kerikeri is justly famous.*

of Whangarei is the home of New Zealand's oil refinery at Marsden Point, named after the first missionary.

Flowers of the North Island

Early settlers had little time to spare for beautifying their pioneer homes, though they brought fruit trees and many plants from Europe.

All around them was the New Zealand bush, thick and luxuriant, and evergreen since the trees are not deciduous. They soon discovered the wealth of flowers that grew there or in more open spaces: the crimson red rata *(Metrosideros robusta)*, a strange but beautiful tree which begins its life as a parasite on a host tree, sending down aerial roots around it towards the ground until it entirely encloses and stifles its host, or the spectacular yellow kowhai *(Sophora tetraptera)*, the delicate white and pink manuka *(Leptospermum scoparium)* which James Cook used to make a medicinal "tea", and above

Russell, Bay of Islands. **Left:** *A launch sets forth for some deep-sea fishing, while* (below) *a family of seagulls reminds the fishermen that they will expect their share of the catch.*

Following pages: *The strange contrasting world of Nature: flowers that bloom like sea anemones, anemonies that have sought refuge in the far corner of a garden, a foxglove shaped like a spire of tiny bells, a dewdrop caught like a magic glass ball on the tip of a succulent's serrated leaf.*

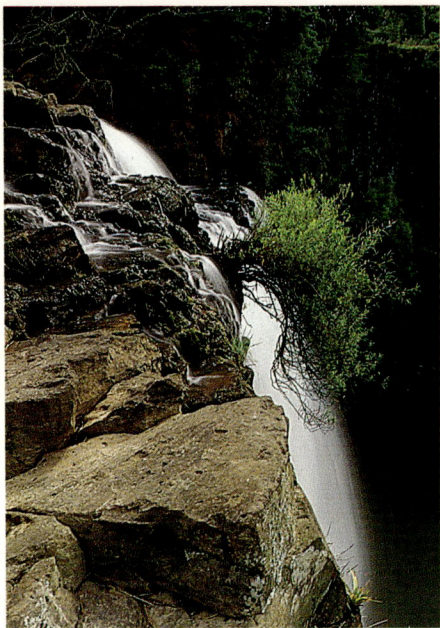

all the pohutakawa *(Metrosideros excelsa)* which they named the Christmas Tree because it blooms in December in a profusion of crimson flowers.

As they became more familiar with their new lands, they learned to understand the Maori's awe of the forest and to discover the wealth of tales that relate to it. The forest lies at the very heart of Maori mythology, for it was Tane, the god of the forest, who had brought the known world into existence. In the dark times, the bodies of Rangi the sky and Papa the earth mother were entwined but Tane planted his head in one and his feet against the other until the mighty bodies were thrust apart and the light flooded in. Tane consoled his father with the stars and adorned the body of his mother with a multitude of trees, the great kauri and the totara, the manuka and the rimu. In the thick, often impenetrable undergrowth, the settlers discovered an abundance of ferns. Soon, indeed, the fern leaf became the national symbol. Ferns range from the

tiny *Hymenophyllum minimum*, which is less than 25 mm high when fully grown, to the mamaku, the tallest fern *(Cyathea medullaris)* which can grow more than 12 m in height and has fronds 5 m long and 2 m wide.

On the plains, they found the strange cabbage tree *(Cordyline australis)* not really a tree but a lily, the tallest in the world, easily reaching 10 to 12 m, and not a cabbage either, but at least with edible roots. If it flowers profusely, in sweet-scented spikes of tiny white flowers, the whole summer, some say, will be hot and dry. And in the marshlands they found the great flax bushes, the *Phormium tenax*, invaluable for the Maori who used it for clothing fabrics, fishing nets, ropes, and which became the basis of a thriving rope industry.

For the North Island is famous for its gardens, private and public. Many plants and flowers have been imported from Britain, reminders of "home" for a few heart-sick immigrants but native shrubs and flowers also have their place in any garden.

Whangarei district. **Left:** *Whangarei Falls.* **Below left:** *A quiet backwater.* **Below right:** *Like an alien in a field of flowers, a roadside letter box awaits the passing mailman. New Zealand letter boxes are famed for their originality and the variety of their design.*

Clockwise: *Kelly Tarlton's Museum of Shipwrecks, Waitangi; Surf breaking, Bay of Islands; the shell-rich beach, Bay of Islands; the oldest stone building in New Zealand, built 1832-35, Kerikeri.*

Natural Wonders

It is a paradox that the centre of the North Island through which runs the Desert Road, across a wind-swept plain of bleak volcanic ash and tussock grass, is one of the richest and most varied parts of the country.

Dominating that desert, the barren legacy of fierce ancient eruptions, Mount Ruapehu and Mount Tongariro, estranged lovers in the old myths, cradle tranquil lakes and a wealth of alpine flowers. It is a mecca for tourists, whether they come to ski, to climb the mountains, to camp and tramp along the mountain paths, or merely to relax and watch the plumes of smoke above the volcanoes from the luxurious haven of the famous Château.

If they look across the tussock, they may glimpse the incongruous shape of a tank or a personnel carrier; for nearby is the large military camp of Waiouru with its Army Museum, a fortress-like building whose architecture brilliantly matches its function and its bleak and barren environment.

But drive along the Desert Road and in less than an hour you will discover Taupo, the country's largest lake, over 600 sq.km in area and 159 m deep through which the longest river flows, the Waikato, which enters it in the south, to re-emerge in the north by the spectacular Huka Falls which boast the largest volume of water of any falls in New Zealand.

A little further on, you pass Wairakei, where steam roars out of the earth, still wildly in parts, but now mostly tamed in order to produce geothermal power. And you have also entered the world's largest man-made forest, covering more than 150,000 hectares and still increasing, the centre of a major timber and paper export industry.

It will serve to remind you that forestry has been an important New Zealand industry from the earliest days of European settlement. Even today 26 percent of the entire country consists of forests.

Drive on through the serried lines of *pinus radiata* and you will emerge in another tourist mecca — Rotorua with its lakes nestled in more forests, and its thermal wonderland where geysers spurt, mud boils

Preceding pages: *Eerie in appearance and dangerous in fact: boiling mud bubbles up in Rotorua.*
Left: *"Tane Mahuta", in the Waipoua forest, believed to be some 1200 years old, is the oldest tree in New Zealand. This giant kauri has a girth of 13.77 m and is estimated to contain 244.5 cubic metres of millable timber.* **Above:** *The Huka Falls, Taupo, a rush of water caused by the Waikato River dropping 8 m over some 230 m of narrow gorge. It is spanned by a narrow footbridge, so that visitors may admire this awesome spectacle.*

ceaselessly and the earth, sulphur-caked, trembles under your feet. Even in the town, steam rises through gratings in the gutters and hot streams trickle along between the long grass by the lakeshore.

Although it is but one of the many in the area, Lake Rotorua is the largest and the best known. In the middle of it there is a famous romantic island, Mokoai, where lived in olden days a youth named Tutanekai. He was in love with Hinemoa, but her people violently disapproved the match.

One evening, hearing the sad notes of Tutanekai's flute over the calm waters, Hinemoa swam across to him and they were at last united. You may still see — and use — the hot spring on Mokoia, named Hinemoa's Pool, where the maiden refreshed herself after her long, cold swim.

But although you may be warned not to attempt to bathe in Waimangu Lake, close by, because however tempting it might appear to be, it is the hottest lake in

he world, with a temperature ranging between 45 degrees and 60 degrees, nevertheless the Rotorua region is a safe area to live.

Its population is rapidly growing, serving the hundreds of thousands of tourists who pass through every year, or simply enjoying its unusual attractions — for where else indeed can you play golf or croquet a few yards away from a boiling stream or with continuous ribbons of steam gently rising out of the earth?

The great canoe of Mata-atua, which so they say brought the *kumara*, the sweet potato, to New Zealand, made its first landfall at Cape Runaway, not far from East Cape, and only a few kilometres from James Cook's Hicks Bay.

Most of this eastern province is spectacular and mountainous country, cut by deep gorges silent but for the ceaseless cascading of the rivers or the calls of the bush birds. From Wairoa in the south, along the peaceful and picturesque Te Mahia Peninsula — which

Preceding pages: *The fearsome thermal world of the North Island. Silica and steam combine in a scene that brings to mind medieval visions of Hell.*

Rotorua's thermal wonderland (below, left) *attracts tens of thousands of visitors each year with its geysers, steam holes, boiling mud and hot streams. The warning, over which a pigeon stands guard* (left), *is not to be taken lightly.* **Below, right:** *A gondola takes tourists up the hill for a view of Rotorua and its lake.*

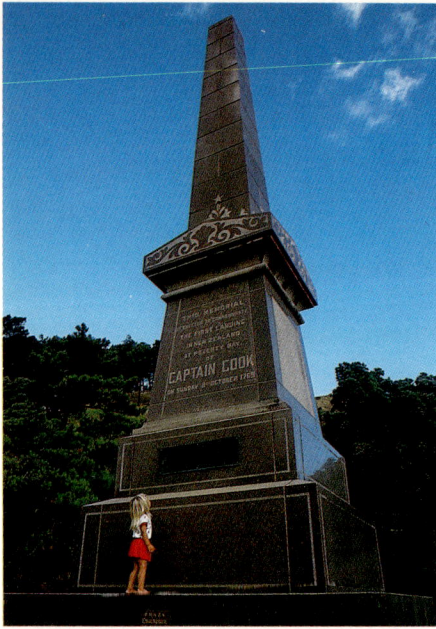

the legends say has magic sand from Hawaiki that attracts whales — up to East Cape and around to Whakatane, the coast is a line of brooding cliffs and silent coves, opening out here and there into a wide plain spreading around a rivermouth, as it does at Gisborne, the largest city, and at Whakatane where Toi the navigator once made his home.

The sea rolls in great waves to the delight of the surfers: the breakers are big for there is nothing to the east but the mighty Pacific and 8,600 km away, the vast unending coast of South America.

This is where the rays of the sun first strike New Zealand each morning, ripening the grapes in the famed Gisborne vineyards, warming the fine sand of the beaches, rousing the birds in their bush nests.

The East Coast is a haven for holidaymakers who fill the camping grounds in the summer, or the more discerning tourists who drive in cooler months through its unspoiled beauty.

Inland, the tree-clad ranges rise in almost endless vistas, the road gently curving around their peaks. Here is the land of the Tuhoe people, the Children of the Mist, the descendants of the Mata-atua settlers, who live in shaded valleys and in settlements well off the beaten track, generally as farmers or forest workers — quiet, hospitable people who still prefer to keep to themselves and preserve their ancient traditions, and simple easy-going way of life in the still and tranquil surroundings of their countryside.

The main road from Wairoa will lead the tourist to the breathtakingly beautiful Lake Waikaremoana, meaning "the Sea of Rippling Waters", 615 metres above sea level, where the dense and rugged bush-covered hills come down to the edge of the water and where dozens of tranquil inlets and bays hold in their quiet shelter a priceless treasure of ancient Maori myths and legends, the entire history of an ancient people enshrined in poetry.

Preceding pages: *Rotorua Croquet Club, a peaceful scene in the Rotorua Public Gardens with the graceful tourist buildings and museum behind. But by moving his camera only a few yards, the photographer could have brought into the picture steam rising from the ground and the hot thermal pools.*

Left: *Monument to commemorate the landing of Captain Cook, Gisborne.* **Below, left:** *Boulders and volcanic soil a few metres from the main road leave no doubt why this part of the central North Island is known as the Desert Road.* **Below, right:** *A rich alpine world nestles among the boulders near Mt Ruapehu.*

Transformed into a stone memorial, but still watchful,
Major Kemp (Te Rangihiwinui Kepa), a Putiki chief
from Wanganui, is framed by a pohutukawa in full
bloom. Kemp won the rare New Zealand Cross in 1876
and was awarded a Sword of Honour by Queen
Victoria. **Above:** *Detail of the pohutukawa flower.*
The pohutukawa is also known as The Christmas Tree
because it flowers late in the year.

Preceding pages: *An unconventional game of cricket on the sands of Makarori Beach near Gisborne.*
Right: *The imagination is given free reign to relieve the factory-made look of mobile homes. Summertime campers relax in a peaceful corner of the East Coast.*

Mount Taranaki

In olden times, Taranaki lived happily among the mountains of the central region until the day when jealous Tongariro who was in love with Ruapehu drove the others away. Taranaki marched off towards the setting sun and now stands a proud and lonely snowy peak over the western plains.

James Cook named him Mount Egmont after the First Lord of the Admiralty, Marion du Fresne named him Pic du Mascarin after his own ship, but to the Maori people it remains loyally Taranaki.

The Taranaki region attracted early settlers who were drawn to its rich soil and who developed a mosaic of dairy farms on the vast surrounding plains.

It is a self-sufficient, somewhat isolated province: the railway lines goes no further than New Plymouth, but those who drive north towards the Mokau River discover a world of quiet fishing settlements and farms.

Its location and its often stormy history have created a distinctive Taranaki character. The people are essentially conservative, individualistic and self-reliant. The "Taranaki gate", a simple contraption of wire and timber, was for many years a symbol of Taranaki ingenuity and independence.

Apart from the port of New Plymouth, it is a region of small towns, each one proud and distinctive. The township of Hawera once declared itself independent from the rest of New Zealand — the "Republic of Hawera" survived for 18 days in 1879 — and it was also the home of New Zealand's most unconventional novelist, Ronald Hugh Morrieson.

Way back in 1866 oil was discovered at Moturoa near New Plymouth. It was the first British oil field. But small as it was, it closed down in 1910 because production exceeded demand; there was no oil refinery, no means of export, and almost no local demand, as there were then scarcely any cars on the roads. It was not until the 1950s that oil exploration began again. And this time it was not plentiful enough for a world which had grown desperate for the product. Later a vast gasfield was found offshore, one of the largest in world and it was named Maui.

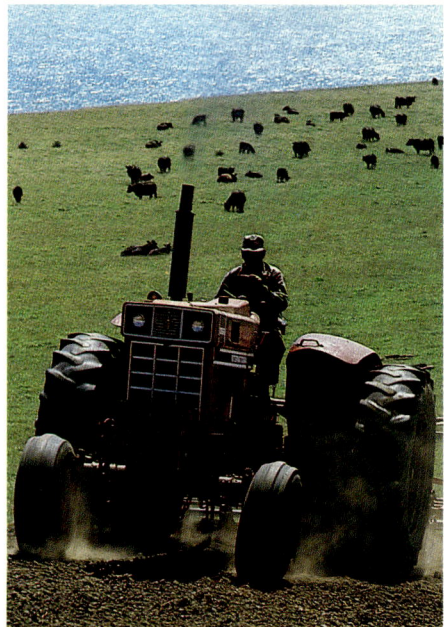

Preceding pages: The quiet charm of a provincial town: Wanganui from Durie Hill.

Taranaki owes its wealth to its rich pastures. **Left:** *The snow-capped cone of Mt Taranaki (known also as Mt Egmont, from the name Captain Cook gave it in 1770) looks down on a familiar scene.* **Above:** *This Taranaki field looks as though it drops straight down into the rippling sea in the background.*

Taranaki contrasts. **Above left:** *The observatory and the haybale outside Pungarehu seem set for a geometrical competition.* **Far left:** *Jim Cash and his trusted tractor outside Pungarehu's small post office.* **Above and left:** *Motunui synthetic fuel plant is based on another source of Taranaki wealth; gas and petrol.*

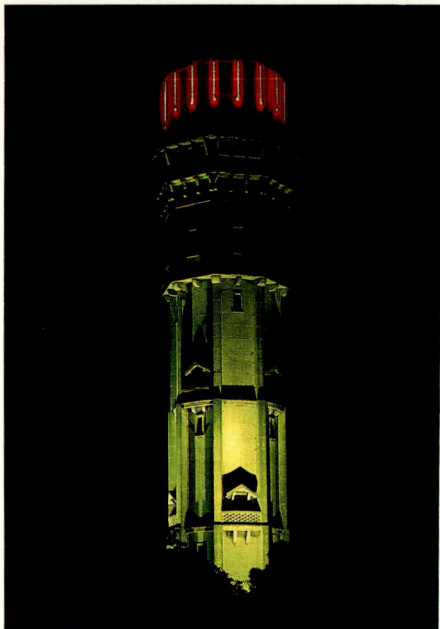

Preceding pages: *An old Taranaki farmhouse resplendent in a sunset that may well be symbolic of its vanishing grandeur.*

Right: *Like a fantasy from outer space, Kapuni natural gas plant glows eerily in the night, its futuristic starkness relieved by the upward-thrusting Norfolk pine.* **Above:** *The water tower, Hawera.*

From Butter to Kiwifruit

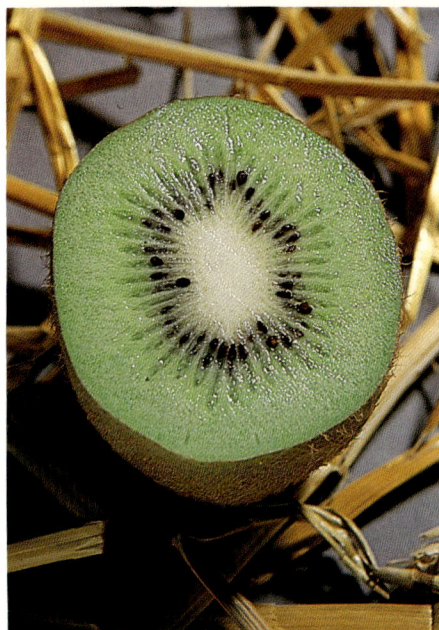

To most people, New Zealand agriculture conjures up an image of sheep and dairy cattle, and to some extent that is a true picture. There are close on 70 million sheep in the country, about 40 million of them in the North Island, and nearly 8 million cattle. New Zealand has in fact 27 times as many domestic animals as there are people — the highest ratio in the world.

The evidence is everywhere. Dairy herds graze on the lush pastures, sheep are everywhere, from the edges of airports where they keep the grass down, to the furthest hills which they cover like a multitude of white dots over green carpets.

Efficient sea transport and above all refrigeration made it all possible. The first refrigerated vessel was a sailing ship, the *Dunedin*, which reached London in 1882. The dairy industry is now highly organised, with gleaming modern cooperative factories producing cheese and butter. Most of the woolclip is sold at auction rooms, where, to the uninitiated, the bidding sounds like the chants and the call of a mysterious ancient ritual. Half of New Zealand's exports still consist of meat, dairy products and wool, all highly competitive on the world market.

Most used to go to Britain, but post-war changes and the advent of the Common Market forced a re-assessment. Dairy farms were ploughed up to produce fruit crops. The Chinese gooseberry, after years of redevelopment, became the large, renamed kiwifruit *(Actinidia chinensis)*, a wonder fruit which produced "kiwifruit millionaires" among those farsighted enough to sense its potential. The strange "tree tomato" was similarly transformed into the highly exportable tamarillo *(Cyphomandra crassifolia)*. Airfreight enabled strawberries and other soft fruit to become luxury winter fruit in the northern hemisphere, while giving rise to a fast-growing canning industry at home.

For a country of beer drinkers — the first "brewery" started operating in the Bay of Islands in 1831, nine years before colonisation — New Zealanders have developed a remarkable wine industry, with production approaching 50 million litres a year.

Preceding pages: The setting sun outlines the silhouette of James Cook's Mt Egmont and the rippling line of its foothills.
Perfect and as simple as any work of art, a brick of butter reflects a New Zealand way of life, while (above) *the elegant artistry of the kiwifruit symbolises new ways and new wealth.*

Introduced to provide sport for the wealthy settlers in the 1850s, deer multiplied rapidly and became a pest, so that millions of dollars had to be spent controlling their number. Now deer farming has become a fast-growing industry. There are close on 150,000 deer grazing on some 1,500 farms behind the special high wire fences that ensure they will not escape into other pastures or back once more into the forests. The story of goat farming has followed the same pattern: introduced by the early settlers for food and weed control, they became a menace; today, a goat industry is developing rapidly, with Angoras fetching prices that hit the headlines.

Introduced in 1814 by an early missionary, Samuel Marsden, horses "caused great amazement among the natives". The extent of the racehorse industry would cause Marsden to be amazed in his turn. Rich grasslands and careful breeding have combined to produce many champions and a $M40 export industry.

Preceding pages: Wherever one goes in New Zealand, one will find sheep, gentle animals in their millions, occupying the landscape as of right. But new shapes have crept in, satellites listening to countries half a world away. Country scene north of Auckland.

Ohakune, a small town just south of Mt Ruapehu, is a developing tourist centre, but it remains at heart a farming town boasting as its emblem the largest carrot in the country. **Below:** *Recently shorn sheep by the woolshed — a central North Island scene, but one which could be repeated a thousand times anywhere in New Zealand.*

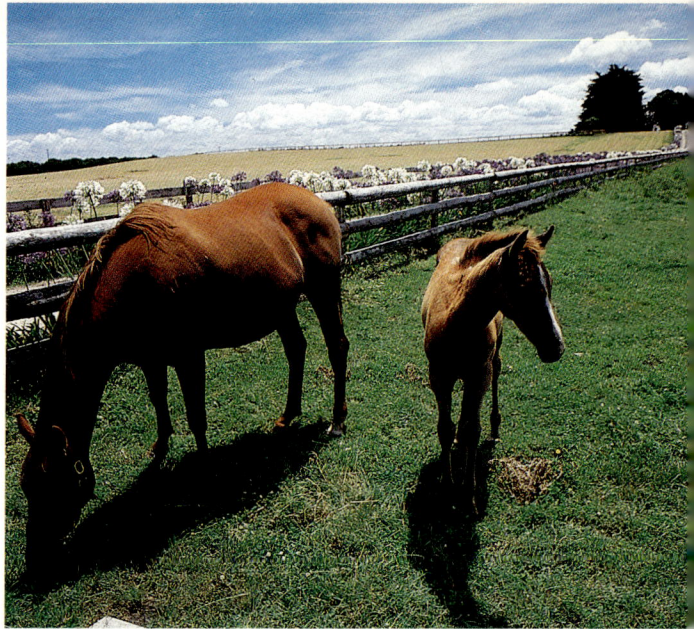

Country scenes. **Clockwise from the left:** *Woolshed against a line of poplars, East Coast. Mother and foal, Wanganui district. Horse and sheep in a back country farm. Mail box, stud farm outside Wanganui.* **Overleaf:** *Exhibiting prize bulls at an Agricultural and Pastoral show calls for concentration and an expert's touch, whether one is wielding a brush or checking a tail for unwanted* **biddy-biddy** *burrs.*

Sacred Places

Europeans found it difficult at first to understand the spiritual practices of the Maori people. It was easier to dismiss them as pagans or animists. The Maoris on the other hand had less trouble in accepting the new concepts the missionaries brought to them, partly because they were the representatives of a wealthy material culture, but also because they offered peace to a people torn by warfare.

But the Maoris were in fact deeply religious people. Their lives were intertwined with the rich Polynesian mythology and a vast array of traditional rituals. While they lacked temples in the narrower meaning of the word, they were surrounded by sacred places: the landing places of the canoes, the burial places of ancestors, natural features — mountains, hills and forests imbued with the spirits of the Polynesian pantheon. Indeed, in the early years of contact, many Europeans unwittingly trespassed into sacred ground or cut a tree protected by a *tapu* — and some paid for their transgression with their lives.

The *marae* was not sanctified ground in the Christian sense. It was a meeting ground, and later a meeting house, protected by a series of important rituals. Even today, in many *maraes,* one does not enter without being formally invited and removing one's footwear.

The largest meeting-house is at Gisborne. It is 41 metres long and 23 metres wide and can accommodate 500 people. The oldest in existence is Te Hau Ki Turanga, built in 1842–3 and lovingly preserved in the National Museum, Wellington.

The Far North has more than its share of historic churches. The smallest surviving church, built of a single kauri tree in Doubtless Bay in 1861, is now in the Whangarei Methodist Museum.

The interaction between Christianity and Polynesian religions led to the rise of a number of Maori sects, some expressing political or local grievances. Most resulted in the erection of chapels or temples, not many of which survive. Rikirangi Te Kooti founded the Ringatu Church which still has its adherents in the Gisborne district.

Preceding pages: Sheep silhouetted in the long grass, near Gisborne, East Coast.

Reconstruction of a Maori pa. Because of frequent inter-tribal warfare, Maori villages were essentially defensive structures, strongly fortified and usually set on a cliffside or steep hill. **Above:** *Carved figure by the top of the palisade. Note the wickedly sharpened points of the stakes.*

Church builders in the main followed traditional European styles. Some churches are clearly inspired by buildings the local minister had been familiar with in England or Scotland, but whatever the preferred style at any one time, the controlling factor was that timber remained the major building material — there is little building stone or granite available in the North Island and bricks present technical problems in earthquake-prone countries. Much of the charm of small country churches results from the tasteful use of timbers.

Symbolic Maori designs appear in a number of churches, and in some, as in Otaki, near Wellington, and in Rotorua, the Maori element dominates in a highly successful artistic blend. The multicultural aspect of modern New Zealand society is reflected in new buildings; not merely the Mormon churches, each patterned on the other, and strikingly white, but also the Samoan churches, Hindu or Buddhist temples and even a Moslem mosque.

Left: Maori meeting house, nineteenth century (Photo, courtesy of Alexander Turnbull Library, Wellington). Below, left: Modern meeting house, with ancient traditional carvings; Putiki marae, Wanganui. Below: Ratana church, south of Wanganui. The Ratana religion is derived from Christianity, but has its own dogmas and ritual. It retains considerable influence among Maoris today.

Following pages: *Bowling Club, Kihikihi. Bowls are played throughout New Zealand on carefully tended grass. No township is too small for a bowling club: Kihikihi's population is just over 1300.*

Warriors, Sailors and Sportsmen

New Zealand's inhabitants acquired very early in their history their reputation as fighters and sailors. It was clear to the first Europeans that the Maoris were a fiercely independent people and highly adept at manoeuvring their long war canoes. How talented they had been as navigators was only realised later when their history became better known.

Living in close-knit groups, they had to defend their territorial rights against others encroaching on their fishing or hunting grounds. They developed great skills as warriors and as builders of fortified villages — skills which still form an integral if symbolic part of Maori culture today.

Until the arrival of the Europeans, the relative strengths of the various tribes were reasonably balanced. The introduction of the musket, although not as murderous a weapon as was once believed, destroyed the balance and caused great social upheavals. In time, the New Zealand warrior, Maori and European, established a new rapport and started to acquire an international reputation.

First bloodied in the Boer war, the New Zealand soldier won his spurs in the First World War. He fought in France and elsewhere, but the major battle was at Gallipoli, a military disaster but a national coming of age. Anzac Day (the word is an acronym of Australian and New Zealand Army Corps) is observed each year as a public day of recollection on 25 April, the anniversary of the 1915 assault on the Turkish-held cliffs.

New Zealanders have taken part in all major wars since those days: in Egypt, Italy and the Pacific during the Second World War, in the Korean War, and in the Vietnam War.

The North Island with its innumerable bays and coves, its quiet beaches, its rivermouths, could not but encourage the growth of a shipping industry. In early days access by sea was much easier and quicker than across the hilly roadless hinterland. This was the way the Maoris had normally communicated, and the

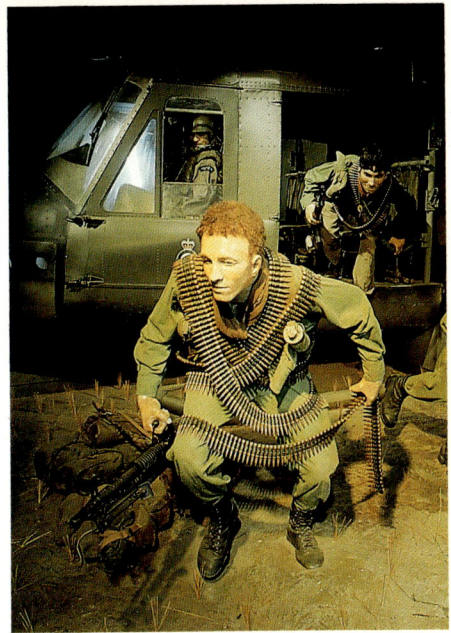

New Zealanders at war. The Army Museum at Waiouru, set near an army camp on the edge of the Desert Road, not only has relics of past wars, but has reconstructed scenes of military life so that future generations can understand what war was really like.

Europeans followed suit, so that ports and small settlements sprang up round the coast. Some of these have turned into great harbours such as at Auckland and Wellington. Others have outgrown their usefulness, until only the remains of a wooden wharf slowly rotting near early buildings remind the tourist of the passing of a once thriving port.

For many years, the British navy saw to New Zealand's defence, but a people so close to the sea soon developed its own naval force, to defend vital shipping lanes against lone raiders stalking the Pacific or to steam further afield to gain glory, as for instance at the Battle of the River Plate in 1939.

But it is the multitude of yachts and small pleasure craft one sees everywhere which provides the real evidence of the New Zealanders' passion for the sea. The annual Auckland regatta on Anniversary Day brings out more than 700 yachts on Waitemata Harbour — more than anywhere else in the world. Less

The wind and the sea. **Below:** *A windsurfer and his board literally fly through the air. Plimmerton, north of Wellington.* **Right:** *Yachts in Auckland Harbour illustrate what is meant by "ploughing the seas".*

Right: *Yacht in harbour, Bay of Islands.* **Above:** *The striped marlin sets off the geometric lines of the deep-sea launch. The fishermen wedge themselves between their seat and the edge of the boat during their struggle against the big fish.*

spectacular no doubt but more original is the yacht race which marks the end of the Wellington season. This is a pub-to-pub race in which contestants, having downed a beer at Clyde Quay tavern, race across the harbour to down a second one at the Eastbourne tavern.

Rugby is undeniably the best known sporting activity in a country famous for its sportsmen. It goes back to 1853 when Christchurch schoolboys played the first game with a bullock's bladder covered in leather. New Zealand's celebrated national team, the All Blacks, so called because of the black jerseys used on their first tour of Britain in 1905, have acquired an unassailable international reputation.

Drive past any town, however small, and you will see the rugby grounds. Indeed, drive past any school playground, whether secondary or primary, whether in a city or a small country settlement, and you cannot fail to notice the tell-tale goalposts, sometimes poised at an unsteady angle.

But cricket is the earliest European game introduced to New Zealand — it was played at the Bay of Islands probably in 1833 and certainly played by men of HMS *Beagle* in 1835. Wellington's first formally organised match dates from 1843, when the settlement was barely three years old, while Auckland and Wellington began their long rivalry with an "inter-provincial" match in 1859. Since then, New Zealand had made its mark in international cricket, winning many epic matches.

Yet the long summer months which might be expected to help cricket, actually work to its detriment. There are simply too many other attractions from November to March. New Zealanders excel at athletics: Jack Lovelock set a world record for the mile in 1933 and broke the 500 metres at the Berlin Olympics, winning New Zealand's first track and field gold medal, Peter Snell broke the 4-minute mile barrier in 1962, John Walker is the first man to reach one hundred sub-4-minute miles, Yvette Williams garnered a rich harvest of gold medals for the long jump, the shotput and the discus.

New Zealand mountaineers acquired world attention when Aucklander Edmund Hillary first climbed Everest, but he is only one of the many thousands of climbers and trampers in New Zealand. Swimming

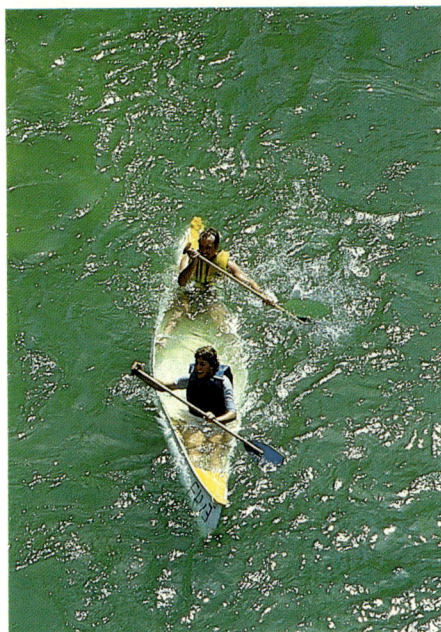

Left: *Proud angler and his catch. Facilities are always available on the wharf to weigh and photograph the catch so that folks back home will not doubt the fisherman's word on his return.* Above: *Half in and half out of the water, canoeists speed on their way over a crystal, transparent sea.*

113

Right: *A champion horse and his proud rider display trophies gained at the Wairoa County Agricultural and Pastoral Show.* Above: *Correct and immaculate dress is an essential requirement for any rider.*

Peter Snell, New Zealand's greatest middle distance runner, first achieved fame winning the 800 m gold medal in record time at the Rome Olympics. The running track in Wanganui where he established another record commemorates his feat. **Right and below:** Touch rugby is a sport for those who still play for fun rather than for fame and who enjoy the atmosphere of a game where rules can still be flexible.

attracts all ages to beaches and swimming pools, and the Surf Lifesavers contests draw attention to the disciplined skills of the thousands of amateur swimmers who patrol the beaches.

Golf has never been the preserve of the rich in New Zealand. There are more than 400 golf clubs including municipally-owned clubs; few have an exclusive membership and none is expensive by world standards. Every town has its bowling club, with immaculate greens and the players of all ages in even more immaculate white.

And horseracing which began with the military in 1840 and was taken over by Aucklanders one year later, has attained national importance and, with champions winning overseas races, international status.

Once a neglected Cinderella, soccer has made astonishing strides in recent years. Soccer clubs have sprung up in every town and most schools now have their football teams and coaches. This success story was

Left: *Rugby players in a line-out concentrating and reaching for the ball in an almost balletic movement.*
Below: *Tension, concentration and determination on every face in a game of softball.*

119

illustrated when New Zealand's national team, the All Whites, reached the last rounds of the World Cup in Spain in 1982.

The farming environment has produced distinctive and unusual sports. Woodchopping contests are common in country districts. Dave Lamberton has won over seventy national contests in chopping and sawing. More obscure but equally cheered on by enthusiastic supporters are those who enter gumboot-throwing competitions, hurling at surprising distances an item of footwear no farmer could do without.

And no visitor could spend more than a few hours in a town or in the countryside without seeing groups of joggers or lonely long-distance runners. Some are training for yet another national or overseas title; most run for pleasure, among them veteran Thelma Pitt-Turner, of Palmerston North, who was still running in marathons in her eighties, probably the oldest contestant in the world.

Saloon car racing along the Wellington waterfront. New Zealanders have acquired an international reputation as racing drivers and in recent years car racing has made great strides on the local scene.

The rodeo, inspired by the traditions of the American West, is popular in many country areas of New Zealand, although the atmosphere is usually more restrained than at a true American rodeo.

Practical Information

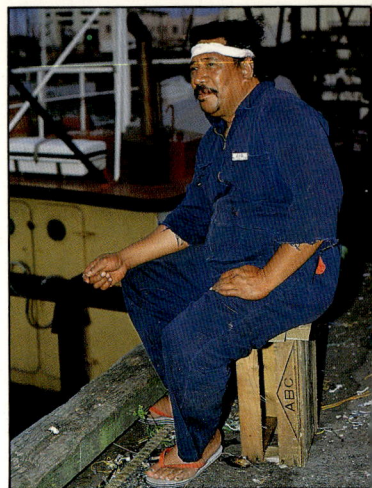

The main International Airport is at Auckland, although flights from Australia operate through Wellington International Airport as well.

For fast internal travel, air transport is advisable, but for more leisurely sightseeing we recommend the use of rental cars or buses, especially as New Zealand has a vast number of comfortable and relatively inexpensive motels. *Newmans* is not only New Zealand's largest and longest established tour operators, but today offers tourists a close network of rental cars, campervans, motor caravans, and travel homes, as well as an internal airline.

The peak holiday period runs from mid-December to mid-February, during which time advance bookings are advisable. Fortunately, the North Island has a particularly mild climate, and travel is easy and pleasant from September to May.

New Zealand has much to offer the outdoor enthusiast: horse-riding holidays, big game fishing along the east coast, trout fishing in lakes and rivers, white water rafting, yachting, skiing and some of the most inexpensive golf courses to be found anywhere.

The thermal region of Rotorua is unique in the world. Bubbling mud pools, boiling geysers, hot lakes and beautiful countryside are features of the area which should not be missed by the tourist eager to experience something different.

Places to See

Northland
Ninety Mile Beach; Waitangi Treaty House; Waipoua Kauri Forest.

Auckland
Museum of Transport and Technology; War Memorial Museum; Kelly Tarlton Aquarium.

Central Area
Waitomo glow-worm caves; Rotorua thermal region; Maori Craft Centre and concert groups; Wairakei Geothermal Power Scheme.

Wellington
Cable Car; Southward Car Museum; Lindale Model Farm.

Tourist Information

Government Tourist Bureau.
P.O.Box 95, Wellington.
Branches in Sydney, Melbourne, Perth, New York, San Francisco, Los Angeles, Vancouver, London, Singapore Tokyo.
Newmans Travel.
P.O. Box 22413, Otahuhu Auckland.
Offices in Sydney, Melbourne Adelaide, Perth, Los Angeles New York, Tokyo, Toronto.
Automobile Association Travel Service.
P.O.Box 1053, Wellington.
Branches throughout New Zealand.
All main towns have a Visitor Information Centre, usually located close to the town hall or the main public library.
Hotel/Motel directories:
AA Accommodation Directory
Jason's Motel Directory.
Tipping: There is no tipping in

New Zealand, whether in hotels or restaurants. Nor are there any local taxes or sales taxes added to any purchases. All marked prices are net.

Climate

New Zealand's climate is temperate, with long sunny hours throughout the country. The prevailing westerly weather pattern means that the entire western coast of the country is exposed, making it excellent for surfing and windsurfing. Being more sheltered, the eastern seaboard is ideal for scuba diving, yachting and fishing. "Down Under", the seasons are the reverse of those in the northern hemisphere, with spring and summer from September to April, autumn and winter from May until end of August. Winter in New Zealand is relatively mild, with the temperatures ranging between 60°F (15°C) to 46°F (8°C), although the Southern Alps has extensive snowfalls during the winter, providing very good skiing.

Electrical appliances

The current throughout New Zealand is 230 volts, 50 hertz. It is an alternating current (AC) so is not suitable for direct current (DC) appliances. Most hotels provide 110 volt, AC sockets for electric razors only.

Water Supply

Throughout the country, the water supply is totally safe.

Foreign exchange, travellers cheques, banks

All trading banks are open from 9.30 am until 4 pm, Monday to Friday, closed on Saturdays, Sundays and public holidays. Credit cards are in wide use throughout the country, in particular, American Express, Visa, Diners Club and Master Charge. Travellers cheques can be changed, at official rates, at trading banks, large hotels in the city and many other facilities in the main cities and top tourist centres.

Souvenirs

Especially interesting is the jewellery made from the famous greenstone — a type of jade, or from the unusual iridescent paua shell. Arts and crafts are a specialty too, from intricate Maori wood carvings or the Tiki, an unusual charm made from greenstone, to the superb woollen sweaters, travel rugs, lambswool rugs and leather goods. Don't forget the excellent — and constantly improving — local wines, and beautifully crafted wooden items like salad bowls, toys, etc.

Emergency

Dial 111 and you will be immediately in touch with police, fire and ambulance in the major centres. Elsewhere, consult the front of the local telephone directory, or a panel provided in all public telephone booths, for information.

North Island

Cape Reinga

Ninety Mile Beach

Bay of Islands
Keri Keri
Russell
Opononi
Poor Knights Islands
Whangarei
Marsden Point
Great Barrier Island
Tokatu Point
Hauraki Gulf
Waiheke Island
AUCKLAND
The Aldermen Island
Shoe 1
Slipper 1

White Island
Cape Runaway
Hicks Bay

HAMILTON
Cambridge
Bay of Plenty
East Cape

Tasman Sea

Whakatane
Ohope Beach
Tokomaru Bay

Rotorua
Waimangu
Lake Rotomahana

Wairakei
Taupo
Lake Waikaremoana
Gisborne

Lake Taupo
Poverty Bay

New Plymouth
▲ Mt. Tongariro
Wairoa
Mahia Peninsula

Pungarehu
Mt. Egmont
Ohakune
Hawke Bay
Napier
Hastings

Wanganui River

Wanganui

PALMERSTON NORTH

Kapiti Island
Porirua Harbour
WELLINGTON

Tory Channel
Palliser Bay
Cook Strait
Cape Palliser

Mike Clare wishes to thank Newman's Rentals New Zealand and
Mobil Oil for their assistance in the making of this book.

Additional photography
Pages 2–3, 20–21, 42–43, 52–53, 66–67, 114–115,
118 – 119, Kal Muller
Pages 22 – 23, 62 – 63, 96 – 97, 122 – 123, Dennis Stock
Pages 6 – 7, 10, 26 – 27, Andris Apse
Pages 58 – 59, 121, Ian Lloyd

Printed in Singapore
Publisher's Number 328